Irresistible Trinidad Recipes

An Enlightening Cookbook on Caribbean Dishes

By

Angel Burns

© 2019 Angel Burns, All Rights Reserved.

License Notices

This book or parts thereof might not be reproduced in any format for personal or commercial use without the written permission of the author. Possession and distribution of this book by any means without said permission is prohibited by law.

All content is for entertainment purposes and the author accepts no responsibility for any damages, commercially or personally, caused by following the content.

Table of Contents

Caribbean Food Recipes 6

Chapter I - Breakfast Recipes 7

    Recipe 1: Saltfish Buljol 8

    Recipe 2: Homemade Trini Cereal 10

    Recipe 3: Plantain Bacon Wraps 12

    Recipe 4: Trinidad Coconut Drops 14

    Recipe 5: Bell Peppers & Sausage 17

Chapter II - Lunch, Dinner and Side Dish Recipes 20

    Recipe 6: Roasted Cauliflower 21

    Recipe 7: Saheena 24

    Recipe 8: Corn Pie 27

    Recipe 9: Stewed Curry Chicken 30

    Recipe 10: Mango Slaw 33

    Recipe 11: Doubles 35

Recipe 12: Cauliflower Fritter.. 38

Recipe 13: Chicken Pelau 41

Recipe 14: Trini Pholourie 44

Recipe 15: Trini Tomato-Avocado Salad.................................. 47

Recipe 16: Mango Curry 49

Recipe 17: Pineapple Chow 52

Recipe 18: Baigan Choka 54

Recipe 19: Trini Macaroni Pie 57

Recipe 20: Trini Fish Broth.. 60

Recipe 21: Cow Heel Caribbean Soup.................................... 64

Recipe 22: Honey Grilled Scotch Bonnet Shrimp 67

Recipe 23: Trini Garlic Dahl 70

Recipe 24: Trinidad Long Beans... 73

Recipe 25: Trini Goat Curry 76

Chapter III - Dessert Recipes.. 80

Recipe 26: Trini Sweet Rice 81

Recipe 27: Banana Fritters 84

Recipe 28: Trinidad Rum Cake 87

Recipe 29: Trini Sugar Cake 90

Recipe 30: Papaya Balls 92

About the Author 94

Author's Afterthoughts 96

Caribbean Food Recipes

HHHHHHHHHHHHHHHHHHHHHHHHHHHHHHHHHH

Chapter I - Breakfast Recipes

HHHHHHHHHHHHHHHHHHHHHHHHHHHHHHHH

Recipe 1: Saltfish Buljol

Although this is intended to be a fish choice for breakfast, you could serve it any time of day. It is popular not just in Trinidad, but also throughout the islands of the Caribbean.

Yield: 3-4 Servings

Preparation Time: 30 minutes

Ingredient List:

- 2 tablespoons of oil, olive
- 1/3 cup of chopped peppers, sweet
- 1/3 of 1 chopped onion
- ½ cup of chopped tomatoes
- ½ pound of boneless salt cod fish
- Black pepper, ground, as desired

HHHHHHHHHHHHHHHHHHHHHHHHHHHHHHHH

Preparation:

1. Break the fish into pieces. Place in a sauce pan with some water. Boil for 10 to 15 minutes and then drain.

2. Taste fish. If it tastes too salty, rinse in water and drain again.

3. Use your fingers to shred the fish.

4. Heat the oil in frying pan. Add the onion. Add in peppers and fish. Fry for one to two minutes.

5. Add tomatoes and mix well. Cook until the tomatoes are barely soft. Add pepper. Squeeze ½ lime over the mixture.

6. Serve with hearty bread, coconut bake or sliced pear.

Recipe 2: Homemade Trini Cereal

It's so simple to mix up your own healthy, tasty cereal without all the additives in boxed cereals. You'll enjoy this recipe, as it is nutritious, filling and tasty.

Yield: 2-4 Servings

Preparation Time: 5-7 minutes

Ingredient List:

- 2 cups of steel cut or rolled oats
- 1/3 cup of blended sesame seeds
- ½ cup of blended flax seeds
- 1/3 cup of sunflower seeds
- 1/3 cup of pumpkin seeds
- 1 & ¼ cup of chopped nuts – may include hazel nuts, cashews, pecans, walnuts or almonds
- 1 cup of fruits, dried – includes cranberries, raisins and dates
- 1 cup of wheat germ

HHHHHHHHHHHHHHHHHHHHHHHHHHHHHHHHH

Preparation:

1. Mix all ingredients together. Store in plastic container and refrigerate.

2. Add cereal mix to a favorite type of milk. Serve.

Recipe 3: Plantain Bacon Wraps

This dish is healthier than many similar recipes. You may use whatever kind of bacon that you prefer. Turkey bacon is a healthy choice. It makes an interesting flavor companion to the sweet plantains.

Yield: 6 Servings

Preparation Time: 15 minutes

Ingredient List:

- Oil, coconut, to fry
- 1 pound of bacon, turkey
- 2 peeled, sliced plantains, ripe

HHHHHHHHHHHHHHHHHHHHHHHHHHHHHHHH

Preparation:

1. Peel & slice the plantains lengthways in ½-inch or slimmer slices. Set them aside.

2. Wrap the plantain slices in turkey bacon. Fry on med. heat. Serve hot.

Recipe 4: Trinidad Coconut Drops

These are traditional drops, unlike those you may find in a bakery. Their texture and taste when homemade far surpass that of those you can buy in a store.

Yield: 4 Servings (8 drops)

Preparation Time: 55 minutes

Ingredient List:

- 1 egg, small
- 1/3 teaspoons vanilla essence
- ¼ teaspoons coconut essence
- 1/3 teaspoons nutmeg
- 1/3 teaspoons cinnamon, ground
- 2 tablespoons of butter, softened
- 1 teaspoon baking powder
- 2 cups of coconut, grated
- ½ cup of brown or granulated sugar
- 1 cup of packed flour, all-purpose

HHHHHHHHHHHHHHHHHHHHHHHHHHHHHHHH

Preparation:

1. Preheat oven to 400F.

2. Sift nutmeg, cinnamon, sugar, baking powder and flour together. Add coconut.

3. Cut in butter. Mix it into flour. Add essences to egg. Beat lightly.

4. Make a well in center of flour. Add liquid. Mix into stiff dough.

5. Drop 2 tablespoons sized dough balls on baking sheet.

6. Lower oven temp to 200F. Bake for 15 minutes. Color should be golden.

7. Remove. Allow to cool. Serve.

Recipe 5: Bell Peppers & Sausage

The bell peppers give this breakfast dish brilliant texture and color. You can use bratwurst sausages or any kind of sausage you enjoy for breakfast.

Yield: 4 Servings

Preparation Time: 35 minutes

Ingredient List:

- 3 thyme sprigs
- 1 garlic clove, crushed
- 1 teaspoon of oil, vegetable
- ¼ teaspoons of pimentón (hot, smoked paprika)
- 3 fresh scallions
- 1 onion, medium, chopped
- 2 medium chopped bell peppers
- 4 turkey sausages
- 1 pinch of salt, sea
- ¼ teaspoons of pepper, black

HHHHHHHHHHHHHHHHHHHHHHHHHHHHHHHH

Preparation:

1. Heat vegetable oil over low heat. Add sausage. Add ½ cup of water to ensure they do not burn. When the water is gone, the sausage is nearly cooked.

2. Turn up heat. Brown outside of sausage. Remove sausage. Set it aside.

3. Add chopped onion and crushed garlic to same pan. Cook over low heat for three to four minutes.

4. Add pimentón, salt, pepper and thyme. Stir to combine. Cook for one minute.

5. Add scallions and bell peppers to mixture. Stir and combine. Mix well so it picks up the flavors from pan bottom that sausage left.

6. Allow to sit for two or three minutes until peppers soften somewhat, yet retain some of their texture.

7. Chop cooled sausages into small pieces. Add back into pan. Save juices and add them to pan, too.

8. Stir and cook for two or three more minutes. Serve hot.

Chapter II – Lunch, Dinner and Side Dish Recipes

HHHHHHHHHHHHHHHHHHHHHHHHHHHHHHHHH

Recipe 6: Roasted Cauliflower

If you don't like the greasiness of some cauliflower dishes, this one's for you. The fried veggies taste irresistible, and it is often enjoyed for lunch with a quinoa salad.

Yield: 2-3 Servings

Preparation Time: 1 hour & 5 minutes

Ingredient List:

- 1 tablespoon + 2 teaspoons of olive oil
- ½ fresh lemon, juice only
- 1 trimmed head of cauliflower with sliced florets
- 1 teaspoon of salt, Himalayan pink
- ¼ teaspoons of pepper, ground

HHHHHHHHHHHHHHHHHHHHHHHHHHHHHHHH

Preparation:

1. Preheat the oven to 450 degrees F.

2. Cut stem from cauliflower.

3. Wash with running water and dry well.

4. Slice the cauliflower florets in halves or thirds for browning.

5. To make the dressing, squeeze lemon juice, and add black pepper, salt and olive oil in large mixing bowl. Whisk until the mixture is cloudy.

6. Add the dressing to the cauliflower florets. Toss and combine.

7. Brush cookie sheet with olive oil.

8. Spread cauliflower in one layer on cookie sheet with flat side facing down.

9. Brush tops of florets with a bit of olive oil.

10. Place pan in oven. Roast until the cauliflower florets are lightly browned. Remove from oven. Allow to cool a bit before serving.

Recipe 7: Saheena

Saheena is made with spinach in a base of split pea flour, which is fried. It's delicious. Most people prefer it made light, or you can make a denser recipe. They are often served with hot pepper sauce or chutney.

Yield: 8-12 Servings

Preparation Time: 1 hour & 20 minutes including 1 hour rising time

Ingredient List:

- 8 minced garlic cloves
- 1 minced onion, medium
- 2 teaspoons of cumin, ground
- 1 tablespoon of powdered curry
- ½ pound of frozen spinach – pre-thawed and excess liquid squeezed out
- 1 pound of flour, all-purpose
- 1 pound of flour, split-pea
- 1 teaspoon of yeast – dissolve with 1 teaspoon sugar in ½ cup water
- Salt, as desired

HHHHHHHHHHHHHHHHHHHHHHHHHHHHHHH

Preparation:

1. Mix the yeast mixture, garlic, cumin, onion, curry powder, salt and flours.

2. Add the chopped spinach. Combine well.

3. Add water. Mix to consistency of soft drops.

4. Set aside to rise for one hour or less.

5. Remove. Drop batter into hot oil.

6. Remove with slotted spoon. Drain on paper towels. Serve.

Recipe 8: Corn Pie

This tasty casserole combines bell peppers and sweet corn in a delicious way. It's a wonderful side dish for parties and times when your family gathers for a feast.

Yield: 6-8 Servings

Preparation Time: 55 minutes

Ingredient List:

- 1 cup of corn meal
- 1 & ¾ cups of cheese
- 1 cup milk, whole
- 3 small cans of corn, cream style
- 1 onion, chopped
- 2 cans corn, whole
- 1 carrot, grated
- 4 chopped cloves of garlic
- ½ cup of chopped parsley
- 4 sticks of chopped chives
- 4 chopped red and yellow peppers
- 1 teaspoon of salt, kosher
- Pepper, ground

HHHHHHHHHHHHHHHHHHHHHHHHHHHHHHHH

Preparation:

1. Place large pot on stove. Heat and add 2 tablespoons oil. Add peppers, garlic, parsley, chive and onions. Let them sauté for several minutes.

2. Add some salt & pepper, carrots and both types of corn to pot. Combine.

3. Add cheese and milk. Mix well. Turn burner off. Add corn meal and mix again. Corn meal gives the pie its nice consistency.

4. Turn stove on. Allow more liquid in pot to dry off for three to five minutes. Transfer mixture to baking dish. Set the oven to 350F.

5. Sprinkle some cheese on top of pie. Bake for 20 to 30 minutes. Allow to cool just a bit. Serve.

Recipe 9: Stewed Curry Chicken

This is a long-time favorite for people who grew up in Trinidad. It is usually served over rice or with a flat bread. You can serve vegetables with it, too.

Yield: 6-8 Servings

Preparation Time: 2 hours & 35 minutes including 2 hours marinating time

Ingredient List:

- ½ diced onion, medium
- 1 chicken, whole, or thigh or breast pieces totaling four to five pounds
- 2 pcs. of thinly sliced pepper, scotch bonnet – use gloves to handle
- 2 tablespoons of sugar, brown
- 1 tablespoon of curry powder
- 4 tablespoons of oil, vegetable
- 5 tablespoons of cilantro
- 1 teaspoon of salt + more if desired
- 1 tablespoon of pepper, black, + more if desired

HHHHHHHHHHHHHHHHHHHHHHHHHHHHHHHHH

Preparation:

1. Cut the chicken into small pieces. Wash with lime juice and water. Rinse and drain.

2. Add cilantro, diced onions, curry powder, salt and pepper. Marinate for two hours or leave overnight.

3. In medium pot, add vegetable oil and 2 slices of pepper. Heat for about three to four minutes.

4. Add brown sugar and allow it to melt, then bubble, then turn dark around edges. If the pot smokes, that's ok.

5. Add seasoned and marinated chicken. Turn and combine with browned sugar. Allow to simmer for five minutes. Turn the chicken. Cover and simmer for five more minutes.

6. Add 1 to 1 & ½ cups of water. Cover and simmer for 10 minutes. Remove the lid. Allow to simmer for about 10 minutes. There should be about two to three spoon-fuls of the thickened liquid in the pan.

7. Remove from heat. Transfer to serving dish. Serve with flat bread.

Recipe 10: Mango Slaw

Try this dish once, and I bet you'll fall in love with it. Be sure to choose mangoes that are neither green nor fully ripe. They should be somewhere in between. This gives you maximum sweetness and they'll still be firm.

Yield: 1-2 Servings

Preparation Time: 15 minutes

Ingredient List:

- Almonds, slivered
- Pepper sauce
- Lime juice, fresh
- ½ onion, red
- ½ red pepper
- Cabbage
- 1 ripe mango
- Sea salt
- Ground pepper

HHHHHHHHHHHHHHHHHHHHHHHHHHHHHH

Preparation:

1. Peel mango, then remove seeds and slice thinly.

2. Cut red pepper, red onion and cabbage thinly.

3. Put onion, mango and cabbage in medium bowl. Squeeze in some fresh lime juice. Add pepper sauce, salt and ground pepper, as desired.

4. Mix all ingredients together with salad tongs. Serve cool.

Recipe 11: Doubles

This is an invention of Trini cuisine. It includes a light bread that sandwiches together tender curried chick peas and mango or tamarind, with a pepper kick.

Yield: 6 Servings

Preparation Time: 1 hour & 10 minutes

Ingredient List:

- 2 chopped onions, green
- 1 pepper, scotch bonnet – handle with gloves
- ½ to 1 teaspoon of pepper, cayenne
- 2 cups + extra broth
- ½ tablespoons of chicken bouillon
- 2 cans of drained chick peas
- 1 teaspoon of cumin, ground
- 2 teaspoons of thyme, dried or fresh
- 1 & ½ teaspoons of paprika, smoked
- 1 teaspoon of nutmeg, ground
- 1 large diced onion
- 1 teaspoon of allspice, ground
- 2 teaspoons of garlic, minced
- 2-3 tablespoons of powdered curry
- ¼ – ½ cup of oil, canola

Curry chick peas:

- 2 tablespoons of parsley, chopped
- ½ teaspoons of salt, kosher + extra as desired
- 1 & ½ teaspoons of pepper, white

HHHHHHHHHHHHHHHHHHHHHHHHHHHHHHHH

Preparation:

1. Heat large pan with the oil. Add curry powder, nutmeg, paprika, allspice, cumin, thyme, garlic and onions. Stir for two or three minutes until the onions are translucent.

2. Add stock.

3. Add green onion, pepper and chick peas. Bring to boil. Allow to simmer until the sauce has thickened. Add parsley. Adjust for consistency, salt and pepper. Serve hot.

Recipe 12: Cauliflower Fritter

These tasty fritters are created by using cilantro, garlic, turmeric, cumin and chick pea flour, plus the cauliflower, of course. They make a delicious and interesting appetizer or you can eat them as a quick snack.

Yield: 4-6 Servings

Preparation Time: 40 minutes

Ingredient List:

- Oil to fry
- ¾ cup of water, filtered
- 1 seeded, diced hot pepper, as desired
- 2 grated garlic cloves
- ¼ cup of onion, chopped finely
- ½ teaspoons of turmeric, ground
- 1 teaspoon of whole cumin, toasted
- ¼ cup of cilantro, chopped
- ½ head rinsed & chopped cauliflower
- 1 cup of flour, chick pea, fine
- 1 teaspoon of sea salt, more or less, as desired

HHHHHHHHHHHHHHHHHHHHHHHHHHHHHHHH

Preparation:

1. Grate garlic, chop the cilantro and the hot pepper. Wash & chop cauliflower.

2. Toasting cumin – Heat small fry pan and add the cumin. Shake it constantly until the cumin becomes aromatic and the color darkens. Remove from the pan. Place on paper towels and allow cooling.

3. Combine salt, hot pepper, garlic, onion, turmeric, cumin, cilantro, cauliflower and flour in large sized bowl.

4. Gradually add in water to make a thick batter. Salt as desired.

5. Heat one inch of oil in fry pan on med. heat.

6. Drop batter in pan using a ¼ cup measurer. Add four at one time. Flatten them with spatula until they are about ½-inch thick.

7. Cook fritters until they brown. Flip and brown other sides. Repeat with the rest of the batter.

8. Remove the fritters and place them on a plate lined with paper towels.

9. Serve alone or with hot sauce or chutney.

Recipe 13: Chicken Pelau

Pelau is a recipe that is often referred as an unofficial traditional dish in Trinidad. It's a one pot meal made with pigeon peas, chicken and rice.

Yield: 4 Servings

Preparation Time: 1 hour & 15 minutes

Ingredient List:

- 1 tablespoon of catsup
- 2 cups of water, filtered
- 2 cups of milk, coconut
- 2 cans of peas, green pigeon
- ½ cup of pumpkin, cubed
- 2 tablespoons of ginger, chopped
- 2 tablespoons of culantro, chopped (similar to cilantro but with stronger aroma)
- 2 chopped garlic cloves
- ½ cup of pimento pepper, chopped (also called flavor pepper)
- ½ cup of onion, chopped
- 5 tablespoons of sugar, brown
- 3 tablespoons of green seasoning (blended spices & herbs)
- 2 tablespoons of parsley, chopped
- 2 pounds of chunk-cut chicken
- 2 tablespoons of salt, kosher
- 2 cups of rice, parboiled
- 2 tablespoons of pepper, ground

HHHHHHHHHHHHHHHHHHHHHHHHHHHHHHHHH

Preparation:

1. Wash chicken and add green seasoning. Set it aside.

2. Heat large pot. Add sugar. Sprinkle evenly on pan bottom.

3. Allow the sugar to become caramelized.

4. Add the seasoned chicken. Stir to coat all the chicken.

5. Cook for between two and five minutes.

6. Drain. Add the pigeon peas. Stir while cooking for about five minutes.

7. Add the rice. Combine well.

8. Add the ketchup, salt, pepper, parsley, ginger, garlic, onion, peppers, pumpkin, water and coconut milk.

9. Bring to a boil before lowering the heat.

10. Simmer for about ½ hour until the rice has cooked partially.

11. Add the culantro.

12. Steam until the rice has fully cooked. Add water if needed. Serve hot.

Recipe 14: Trini Pholourie

Ah, these sweet fried balls made from split-pea flour. They are made in roughly the same size as doughnut holes, and you can glaze them with tamarind or mango.

Yield: 4-5 Servings

Preparation Time: 50 minutes

Ingredient List:

- 1 & 1/3 cups of water, warm, for making batter
- ½ teaspoons of powdered curry
- 2 green onions - chopped white portion only
- 2 to 3 tablespoons of chopped onion
- ½ teaspoons of turmeric
- ½ minced scotch bonnet pepper- - handle with gloves on
- 1 tablespoon of cilantro
- ½ teaspoons of cumin
- 3 or 4 cloves of garlic
- 2 teaspoons of yeast
- ½ cup of flour, split-pea
- 2 cups of flour, all-purpose
- 1 teaspoon of sea salt, + extra as desired
- 2 teaspoons of sugar, granulated
- Vegetable oil

HHHHHHHHHHHHHHHHHHHHHHHHHHHHHHHHH

Preparation:

1. Blend scotch bonnet pepper, onions, garlic and cilantro in food processor until they are pureed.

2. Combine yeast, onion mix, curry, turmeric, cumin, sugar, salt, both types of flour and water in large bowl. Mix well.

3. Add the warm water in a bit at a time 'til consistency is as you desire. It is usually similar to a thick pancake batter.

4. Set mixture in warm area of your house. Allow to rise. It will double in size in about one to two hours.

5. Pour veggie oil in large saucepan, until three inches high. Heat at medium until the oil temperature is 375F or so.

6. The dough will be sticky, so grab a bit of the mixture, using your hands and form balls. Drop carefully in oil. Don't put too many in at once – fry them in batches.

7. For each batch, fry for seven to eight minutes until bottoms of balls are lightly browned. Turn balls over and fry on other side.

8. Remove balls from oil with slotted spoon. Place on paper towels to soak up any excess oil. Serve warm.

Recipe 15: Trini Tomato-Avocado Salad

If you mince the ingredients for this recipe in a food processor, it helps them to blend together especially well. Once you mix them in, the tomatoes and avocados are coated with a tasty blend consisting of cilantro, garlic and red onion.

Yield: 2-3 Servings

Preparation Time: 15 minutes

Ingredient List:

- 1 tablespoon of oil, olive
- 1 tablespoon of lemon juice, fresh
- 1 garlic clove
- 1 tablespoon of minced cilantro, fresh
- 2 tablespoons of minced onion, red
- 1 diced tomato, medium
- 1 peeled, diced and pitted avocado, small
- Sea salt, as desired
- Black pepper, as desired

HHHHHHHHHHHHHHHHHHHHHHHHHHHHHHHHH

Preparation:

1. Sprinkle the lemon juice on diced avocado to reduce oxidation and browning.

2. Mince garlic, cilantro and red onion in food processor.

3. Combine the garlic, cilantro, red onion, tomato and avocado in large bowl. Add salt & pepper as desired.

4. Drizzle using olive oil. Serve promptly.

Recipe 16: Mango Curry

Can you make curry with a fruit? Indeed, you can, and you will even use the seeds and skin. The mango curry can be served as a standalone side dish or with other types of curry.

Yield: 4 Servings

Preparation Time: 55 minutes

Ingredient List:

- 3 garlic cloves
- 2 tablespoons of oil for cooking
- 1 tablespoon of powdered curry
- 4 or 5 long mangoes, green
- Sea salt & ground pepper, as desired

HHHHHHHHHHHHHHHHHHHHHHHHHHHHHHHH

Preparation:

1. Wash the mangoes and dry them. Cut off the stem ends. Chop in half. Then cut like you would an orange (lengthways) and set them aside.

2. Mix ½ cup of cold water with 1 tablespoon of curry powder, forming a paste.

3. Pour 1 tablespoon of oil in large pot. Add curry paste. Cook while stirring on low heat until you cook out all the starch.

4. Add the mango to pot. Stir until it is coated with the curry paste.

5. Add 2 crushed garlic cloves, ½ cup of water, salt and pepper.

6. Cover. Cook 'til tender. Serve.

Recipe 17: Pineapple Chow

There is something magical about combining fresh fruit chunks with garlic, salt, hot pepper and lime juice. The result does not look like a dish worthy of a photo op, but it is sweet and has a kick at the same time.

Yield: 2-3 Servings

Preparation Time: 1 hour & 25 minutes including 1 hour sitting time

Ingredient List:

- 2 chopped chilies, red
- ¼ teaspoons of chopped garlic
- 1 tablespoon of chopped cilantro
- 1 cup of ripe pineapple
- Salt, kosher, as desired

HHHHHHHHHHHHHHHHHHHHHHHHHHHHHHHH

Preparation:

1. Cube the pineapple. Chop the cilantro, hot peppers and garlic.

2. Add cilantro, salt, garlic, peppers and pineapple to a bowl and blend.

3. Allow the mixture to sit for about an hour, so the flavors can blend. Serve chilled.

Recipe 18: Baigan Choka

The eggplant in Baigan Choka is fire-roasted and mashed with tasty browned bits of garlic, onion and pepper. It is sometimes prepared with red tomatoes or okra.

Yield: 4 Servings

Preparation Time: 25 minutes

Ingredient List:

- 2 teaspoons of oil, olive
- ¼ cup of chopped onion
- 1 seeded and sliced tomato, medium
- 4 cloves of garlic
- 1 eggplant, large

HHHHHHHHHHHHHHHHHHHHHHHHHHHHHHHHHH

Preparation:

1. Wash the eggplant. Slit it with knife.

2. Peel cloves of garlic. Stick into eggplant slits you just made.

3. Stick wedges of tomato into slits, as well.

4. Rub eggplant with oil.

5. Roast over open flame until it is soft. Don't grill.

6. When the eggplant becomes soft, slit charred skin lengthwise and scrape out stringy, soft pulp. Discard the skin.

7. Mash that pulp, along with garlic and tomato in bowl or blender.

8. Add 1 teaspoon of olive oil to fry pan. Cook onion until it is fragrant, but NOT long enough that it becomes translucent.

9. Add onion to eggplant pulp and salt as desired. Serve with flat bread.

Recipe 19: Trini Macaroni Pie

This pie is used quite often as a comfort food. It is somewhat similar to a casserole of baked mac and cheese, but this is baked before the cheese is melted.

Yield: 8 Servings

Preparation Time: 55 minutes

Ingredient List:

- 3 & ½ cups of cheddar cheese, grated
- 1 teaspoon of thyme, dried
- 1 & ½ teaspoons of mustard powder, dry
- 1 teaspoon of garlic powder
- 2 & 2/3 cups of milk, evaporated
- 3 eggs, large
- ¼ cup of chopped onion
- 1 tablespoon of butter, salted
- 2 cups of macaroni, uncooked
- 1 pinch cayenne pepper
- 1/3 teaspoons of salt, kosher
- ¼ teaspoons of pepper, white

HHHHHHHHHHHHHHHHHHHHHHHHHHHHHHH

Preparation:

1. Preheat the oven to 350F.

2. Grease 11x9-inch baking dish. Set it aside.

3. Boil macaroni using instructions on package. After it has cooked, drain it. Place back in pot off heat, to cool.

4. Melt the butter in a frying pan on med. heat. Add the onions and cook until they are slightly caramelized and softened. Scrape melted butter and onions into macaroni pot. Combine by stirring.

5. Beat the eggs until they are fluffy, in large bowl. Add the cayenne pepper, thyme, mustard powder, garlic powder, salt, pepper and milk. Stir well to combine.

6. Pour egg mixture over macaroni. Stir until the pasta is coated well.

7. Stir in three cups of cheese shreds.

8. Pour in 11x9-inch baking dish. Top with remainder of cheese shreds.

9. Bake for about 35 to 40 minutes.

10. Allow the pie to sit for 10 to 15 minutes. Serve.

Recipe 20: Trini Fish Broth

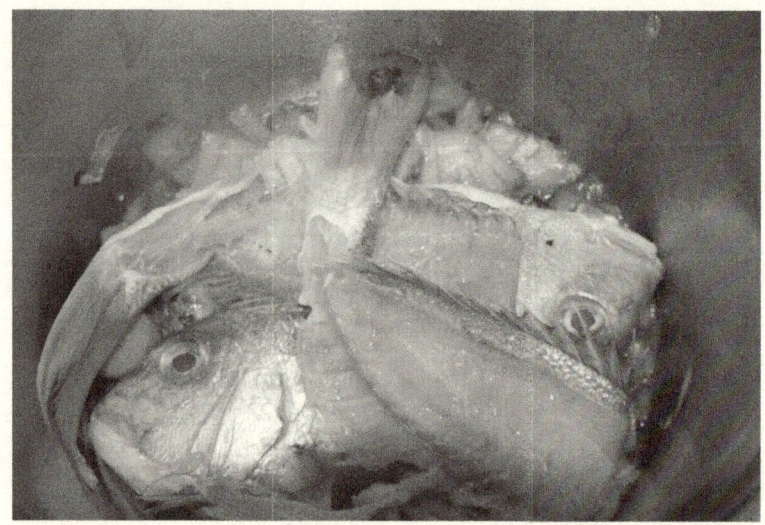

Broth sounds rather boring, doesn't it? This one is not. It has a delicate and traditional Trinidadian flavor from its herbs, garlic, root veggies and fish.

Yield: 6-8 Servings

Preparation Time: 2 hours & 3 minutes including 1 hour of marinating time

Ingredient List:

- 6 garlic cloves, large
- Prepared flour dumplings
- 4 chopped scallions, large
- 6 to 8 minced culantro (bandania) leaves (this is different than cilantro)
- Green seasoning (spice, herb mix)
- 3 tablespoons of lime juice, + extra for serving
- 4 thyme sprigs
- 3 tablespoons of ketchup, organic, + extra for serving
- 1 whole pepper, hot
- 1 sliced tomato, medium
- 1 sliced & chopped in one-inch pieces celery stalk
- 1 peeled, sliced onion, large
- 2 lbs. of small fish or fish slices – red fish, snapper or croaker
- 3 peeled eddoes (tropical taro), small
- 6 to 8 ochroes (okra) – remove tops
- 1 sliced carrot, medium
- 2 peeled, quartered figs
- 1 to 3 peeled, quartered sweet potatoes
- 1 peeled, quartered potato, large
- 3 quarts of water, filtered

- 1 fresh lime, juice only, to wash fish
- Sea salt & ground pepper, as desired

HHHHHHHHHHHHHHHHHHHHHHHHHHHHHHHHH

Preparation:

1. Wash, peel & cut the veggies. Slice the onion and tomato.

2. Leave the root vegetables in water so they won't turn black.

3. Mince the culantro, scallions and garlic in food processor.

4. Soak fish in lemon juice and water for several minutes. Check for any scales, then rinse and drain the fish.

5. Season the fish with ½ green seasoning, salt and pepper. Marinate for one hour or leave overnight.

6. Bring water to a boil in covered pot on high heat.

7. Add remaining green seasoning, along with hot pepper, thyme, celery, tomato, onion, eddoes, carrot, figs, sweet potato and onion.

8. Bring back up to boil. Cover. Lower heat to a low setting. Cook until the veggies are firm but fork tender. This will take between 20 and 40 minutes.

9. Season as desired with salt and pepper.

10. Add the fish to your pot. Cover. Cook for five minutes or so. Don't stir.

11. Add the dumplings. Bring heat up to high. Bring soup to boil. Reduce heat and allow the dumplings to cook.

12. Add ketchup and lime juice. Stir pot contents gently. Adjust taste as desired. Remove thyme sprigs and hot pepper. Serve hot.

Recipe 21: Cow Heel Caribbean Soup

Cow heel doesn't sound appetizing, but it most certainly is, in this dish. It has a texture like chicken ligaments, but the fig, potato, carrot and dumplings are coated in a flavorful broth that is truly amazing.

Yield: 4-5 Servings

Preparation Time: 1 hour and 10 minutes

Ingredient List:

- 2 cut carrots
- 12 prepared dumplings
- 6-8 okra
- ½ cup of split peas, yellow
- 1 cup of diced onions
- 2 teaspoons of oil, olive
- 2 lbs. of cut up cow heel
- 6 thyme sprigs
- Salt, as desired
- Pepper, as desired

HHHHHHHHHHHHHHHHHHHHHHHHHHHHHHHH

Preparation:

1. Use a pressure cooker for this recipe. It will help the cow heel to become tender.

2. Heat the oil in the pressure cooker.

3. Add thyme and onions. Sauté until onions become translucent.

4. Add the cow heel, salt & pepper. Sauté with thyme and onions.

5. Add five cups of water and stir mixture. Cover. Allow to cook for ½ hour.

6. Release pressure valve to release steam. Open and add peas plus additional water. Water should be sufficient to make soup and cook peas.

7. Add the thyme. Let cow heel and peas cook over high heat.

8. Add dumplings and okra. Cover. Allow to cook for six to eight minutes. Taste and adjust seasoning as desired. Stir. Serve.

Recipe 22: Honey Grilled Scotch Bonnet Shrimp

This dish sounds intimidating, but actually, it's quite easily prepared. It offers Caribbean flavor in each bite. The honey balances the hot kick of the scotch bonnet pepper.

Yield: 4 Servings

Preparation Time: 1 hour & 20 minutes including 1 hour of marinating time

Ingredient List:

- 1 finely chopped scallion
- 1 teaspoon of garlic, minced
- 2 diced scotch bonnet peppers – handle with gloves
- 2 tablespoons of oil, olive
- 2 tablespoons of honey, pure
- 1 lb. of peeled, de-veined shrimp, large
- 1 pinch sea salt

HHHHHHHHHHHHHHHHHHHHHHHHHHHHHHHHH

Preparation:

1. Remove white membrane and seeds from scotch bonnet peppers before dicing if you don't want raw heat in the dish.

2. Place cleaned shrimp and remaining ingredients in a zip-top bag. Toss it a bit and store in your refrigerator for about an hour.

3. Thread shrimp on skewers. Prepare a hot grill or a grill pan on stove.

4. Grease grill surface. Place skewers over med-low heat for three to four minutes on the first side.

5. Flip and cook for a couple of minutes on the other side. Do not overcook.

6. Squeeze on lemon juice. Serve.

Recipe 23: Trini Garlic Dahl

Dhal is easily made, and the ingredients are easy to find and inexpensive, as well. It is most often served with rice or naan bread. Either way, it's a delicious taste of the islands.

Yield: 2 Servings

Preparation Time: 1 hour & 10 minutes

Ingredient List:

- ½ teaspoons of turmeric
- ¼ of 1 scotch bonnet pepper – handle with gloves
- 1 onion, very small
- 3 garlic cloves
- 5 cups of water
- 1 cup of peas, split
- Salt, pink Himalayan
- ½ teaspoons of pepper, black

For the mixing (chongkaying):

- 1 teaspoon of cumin, ground
- 2 to 3 garlic cloves
- 2 tablespoons of oil, coconut

HHHHHHHHHHHHHHHHHHHHHHHHHHHHHHHH

Preparation:

1. Rinse split peas well. Pour into sauce pan on med-high.

2. Add water, pink salt, onions, garlic, pepper, scotch bonnet and turmeric to pot.

3. Bring pot to boil. Cover. Lower heat to med-low.

4. Allow split peas to sit and simmer for 40 minutes until they are tender.

5. Once peas soften, remove pot from heat. Pulverize mixture. Stir.

6. For mixing, melt coconut oil in fry pan. Add cumin and garlic. Transfer ingredients into dhal. Stir to combine. Serve promptly.

Recipe 24: Trinidad Long Beans

This long bean (bodi) recipe includes long (green) beans that are stir fried with garlic, tomatoes and onions. Cook it beyond its steaming point to bring out the most intense flavor.

Yield: 2-4 Servings

Preparation Time: 40 minutes

Ingredient List:

- 2 tablespoons of oil, olive
- 3 crushed cloves of garlic
- 1 sliced onion, medium
- 1 or 2 diced tomatoes, medium, ripe
- 1 bunch of trimmed, washed and cut green beans, long
- Salt, kosher, as desired

HHHHHHHHHHHHHHHHHHHHHHHHHHHHHHHHH

Preparation:

1. Wash beans. Drain. Wash repeatedly until water runs clear. Drain each time.

2. Trim tops with knife.

3. Cut into pieces of one to two inches each.

4. Cut onion and tomatoes. Pound or crush garlic into small pieces.

5. Heat 2 tablespoons of oil in heavy pot on med. heat. Add garlic, onion and tomatoes.

6. Stir-fry for several minutes.

7. Add long beans and some salt. Stir-fry on med-high.

8. Beans are done when they start turning brown and shriveling up. This takes between 10 and 15 minutes. Serve at room temp. or hot.

Recipe 25: Trini Goat Curry

You may think that goat meat is always gamey and tough. Put those beliefs aside and try this Trini goat recipe. The meat is tender and captures all the sauce, and it's so tasty you won't believe it's goat meat.

Yield: 6 Servings

Preparation Time: 1 hour & 5 minutes + 2 days marinating time

Ingredient List:

- 3 & ½ ounces of butter, softened
- 7 ounces of coconut, block
- 1 tablespoon of sugar, light brown
- 5 tablespoons of rum, dark
- 2 & ¼ pounds of cubed goat meat
- 3 cloves
- 2 cinnamon sticks
- 2 to 3 tablespoons of oil, coconut
- ¼ teaspoons of allspice
- 2 tablespoons of celery, chopped
- 1 chopped onion
- 2 chopped carrots, medium
- 2 diced tomatoes
- 1 & 1/3 quarts of stock, beef
- 3 to 4 bay leaves
- 3 chopped onions, spring
- 3 sprigs of oregano, fresh
- 4 thyme sprigs, fresh
- 5 chopped garlic cloves
- ½ tablespoons salt, kosher
- ¼ teaspoons pepper, black

For curry paste:

- 1 chopped scotch bonnet pepper – use gloves to handle
- 2 tablespoons of coriander powder and cumin
- 1 teaspoon of powdered turmeric
- 2 tablespoons of curry powder
- 2 tablespoons of ginger and garlic paste
- ½ onion, medium
- 1 bunch of coriander, fresh

HHHHHHHHHHHHHHHHHHHHHHHHHHHHHHHH

Preparation:

1. Cover goat meat with rum, oregano, thyme, spring onions, bay leaves and garlic in large-sized bowl. Allow to marinate for two days.

2. Place meat and all marinade in pressure cooker with stock, tomatoes and onion. Cook for about 40 minutes.

3. Add salt, pepper, allspice, celery and carrots to stew. Set it aside.

4. Melt coconut oil on med-high. Add cloves and cinnamon. Temper spices in oil for one minute or so.

5. Add 1 tablespoon of lt. brown sugar. Stir until it has caramelized. It should appear much darker, but don't allow it to burn and blacken.

6. Pour in stew. Allow to simmer.

For curry paste

7. Blend all curry paste ingredients and form a fine paste. Pour it in pan with sauce.

8. Add coconut. Allow to melt. Add butter. Stir until it melts in sauce. Check and adjust seasonings. Combine and serve hot.

Chapter III - Dessert Recipes

HHHHHHHHHHHHHHHHHHHHHHHHHHHHHHH

Recipe 26: Trini Sweet Rice

Trinidadians call their rice pudding "sweet rice". It's another dessert that is very popular in the Caribbean islands. The rice will be cooked with spices, three kinds of milk and ginger, creating a creamy, classic pudding.

Yield: 1-2 Servings

Preparation Time: 45 minutes

Ingredient List:

- 2" piece of grated ginger
- 1 can of milk. condensed
- 1 cup of evaporated milk
- 1 teaspoon of cinnamon, ground, as desired
- 1 cup of whole milk, organic
- 4 cups of water, filtered
- 1 cup of white rice, uncooked

HHHHHHHHHHHHHHHHHHHHHHHHHHHHHHHH

Preparation:

1. Wash the rice several times, changing water until it runs clear. Drain the rice.

2. Add ginger, cinnamon, rice and water to stock pot. Bring uncovered to boil on high heat. Once it boils, reduce heat immediately to medium.

3. Cook until the rice is tender and water has been absorbed. If not yet soft, add more water and continue cooking until it's done.

4. Add the whole milk. Cook until most of it has been absorbed. Turn often so it won't stick.

5. Add the evaporated milk. Stir continuously while cooking until the milk cooks down.

6. Add the condensed milk. Stir while cooking until it thickens but has not yet evaporated. Serve cold or hot, with fruit or alone.

Recipe 27: Banana Fritters

Banana Fritters are known as "gulgula" in Trinidad. They are simple but tasty treats that came from the ancestors of Trinidadians, immigrants from India, who came originally to Trinidad to work on the many sugar cane plantations.

Yield: about 20 Servings

Preparation Time: 40 minutes

Ingredient List:

- Oil to fry
- 1 pinch of cinnamon, ground
- ¼ cup of sugar, brown
- 1 teaspoon of baking powder
- 1 cup of flour, all-purpose
- 3 bananas, very ripe
- ½ teaspoons of salt, kosher

HHHHHHHHHHHHHHHHHHHHHHHHHHHHHHHHHH

Preparation:

1. Mash the bananas with a fork.

2. Combine cinnamon, salt, brown sugar, baking powder and flour in medium bowl.

3. Add bananas. Combine the mixture until it is smooth.

4. Heat oil up to 2 inches in small fry pan on med. heat.

5. Create small balls in batter by moving with two spoons and scooping up.

6. Drop heaping balls of batter carefully in hot oil, in batches.

7. Turn once while frying, until lightly browned on all sides.

8. Use a slotted spoon to transfer balls to paper towels on a pan.

9. Allow to rest for a couple minutes. Serve.

Recipe 28: Trinidad Rum Cake

The Caribbean islands have always been famous for rum and the recipes that use it so well. This rich cake recipe is a must for lovers of wine. It is often served on birthdays and holidays.

Yield: 12 Servings

Preparation Time: 1 hour & 45 minutes

Ingredient List:

- ½ teaspoons of cinnamon, ground
- 2 & ½ cups of flour, all-purpose
- ½ teaspoons of allspice, ground
- 3 teaspoons of baking powder
- ½ teaspoons of nutmeg, ground
- 1 cup of molasses, dark
- 2 cups of wine, red
- 2 lbs. of fruit, mixed, dried, chopped
- 1 fresh lime, zest only
- 1 tablespoon of almond extract
- 1 teaspoon of vanilla extract
- 1 tablespoon of lime juice
- ¼ cup of rum, white
- 2 cups of sugar, granulated
- 9 medium eggs
- 2 cups of butter, unsalted
- 1 pinch of sea salt

HHHHHHHHHHHHHHHHHHHHHHHHHHHHHHHH

Preparation:

1. Preheat the oven to 350F.

2. Grease & flour two x 9" cake pans.

3. Cream together sugar and butter in large mixing bowl until fluffy and light. Beat in the eggs. Add the lime zest, almond extract, vanilla, lime juice and rum.

4. Stir in the molasses, mixed fruit and wine.

5. Sift salt, cinnamon, allspice, nutmeg, baking powder and flour together. Fold it into a batter, but don't overmix it. Pour into the greased, floured pans.

6. Bake in oven for 80-90 minutes. Allow to cool for 10 minutes in the pan. Turn out on a wire rack to finish cooling. Serve.

Recipe 29: Trini Sugar Cake

This dessert is made in the form of coconut and sugar candy. If you have a sweet tooth, you will truly love it.

Yield: 15 Servings

Preparation Time: 35 minutes

Ingredient List:

- 1 teaspoon of almond extract
- ½ teaspoons of cream of tartar
- 4 cups of unsweetened coconut, shredded
- 1 cup of water, purified
- 4 cups of sugar, granulated
- Optional: food coloring

HHHHHHHHHHHHHHHHHHHHHHHHHHHHHHHHHH

Preparation:

1. Boil water and sugar. They will form a light-colored syrup.

2. When you can see small bubbles, add cream of tartar and grated coconut.

3. When you can remove the coconut mixture easily, without any syrup running out, remove from heat. Use a spoon to beat for three to five minutes.

4. Add food coloring, if using, and almond extract.

5. Drop balls of mixture on a tray to make sugar cakes. Allow to cool. Serve.

Recipe 30: Papaya Balls

Also called paw paw balls, these are homemade candy desserts that are deceptively simple to make. Everyone in Trinidad loves them, it seems. From tourists to lifetime residents, it's a much-welcomed treat.

Yield: 4-6 Servings

Preparation Time: 25 minutes

Ingredient List:

- ¾ cup of sugar for each papaya cup
- 2 teaspoons of lime juice
- 1 teaspoon of zest, lime
- 1 peeled, grated papaya
- Red or green food coloring

HHHHHHHHHHHHHHHHHHHHHHHHHHHHHHHHH

Preparation:

1. Squeeze any excess juice from grated papaya.

2. Measure papaya in cups. Add ¾ cup of sugar for each cup of papaya.

3. Mix lime juice, lime zest, sugar and papaya in pan.

4. Slowly cook on med-low until mixture has gelled.

5. Add several drops of green or red food coloring. Allow to cool.

6. Shape into balls. Roll them in the granulated sugar. Serve.

About the Author

Angel Burns learned to cook when she worked in the local seafood restaurant near her home in Hyannis Port in Massachusetts as a teenager. The head chef took Angel under his wing and taught the young woman the tricks of the trade for cooking seafood. The skills she had learned at a young age helped her get accepted into Boston University's Culinary Program where she also minored in business administration.

Summers off from school meant working at the same restaurant but when Angel's mentor and friend retired as head chef, she took over after graduation and created classic and new dishes that delighted the diners. The restaurant flourished under Angel's culinary creativity and one customer developed more than an appreciation for Angel's food. Several months after taking over the position, the young woman met her future husband at work and they have been inseparable ever since. They still live in Hyannis Port with their two children and a cocker spaniel named Buddy.

Angel Burns turned her passion for cooking and her business acumen into a thriving e-book business. She has authored several successful books on cooking different types of dishes using simple ingredients for novices and experienced chefs alike. She is still head chef in Hyannis Port and says she will probably never leave!

Author's Afterthoughts

With so many books out there to choose from, I want to thank you for choosing this one and taking precious time out of your life to buy and read my work. Readers like you are the reason I take such passion in creating these books.

It is with gratitude and humility that I express how honored I am to become a part of your life and I hope that you take the same pleasure in reading this book as I did in writing it.

Can I ask one small favour? I ask that you write an honest and open review on Amazon of what you thought of the book. This will help other readers make an informed choice on whether to buy this book.

My sincerest thanks,

Angel Burns

If you want to be the first to know about news, new books, events and giveaways, subscribe to my newsletter by clicking the link below

https://angel-burns.gr8.com

or Scan QR-code

Made in the USA
Las Vegas, NV
22 December 2023